TIME AND MOTION

Inscribed for Simon,
with fellow-feeling!
(Arvon, April 1981)

Sylvia.

14, Osborne Parc,
Helston,
Cornwall.

TIME & MOTION

SYLVIA KANTARIS

First published in the PRISM series
by New Poetry for the Poetry Society of Australia, 1975.
Reprinted in Great Britain, 1980.

This book is copyright.

Apart from any fair dealing for the purposes of private study, research, criticism or review as permitted under the Copyright Act, no part of this publication may be reproduced, stored in a retrieval system or transmitted in any form or by any means, electronic, mechanical, photocopying, recording or otherwise without prior permission of the copyright owner.

© Sylvia Kantaris

Cover Art by Kay Whitehead

ISBN 0 85869 007 1

CONTENTS

CONTENTS

Acknowledgement is made to

The Australian
Australian Letters
Beyond Poetry
New Poetry
Orbis (England)
Ostrich (England)
Overland
Poetry Australia
Poetry Magazine
Southerly

Time and Motion

Once upon a time, time
had a woman's shape,
and men could lay an hour-glass on the sand
and stop time horizontally with love, still,
or set the sands in motion at their will
to fill an hour before the next oasis.
Clocks stop for no man,
only for themselves, at the
wrong times. Helplessly
we revolve on a clock face,
making love clockwise,
timing eggs.

Commuter

He was the husband.
He lodged in the house of the wife,
triangularly.
His mapped itinerary from
study to drawer to
bedroom drawer to
kitchen shelf
had left him ignorant
of all the messy cupboards
on the borders of his route.
The wife knew.
The house was hers.
All the half-melted mothballs of her life
were hidden there, unfiled,
but polished daily,
for fear the dust should eat them all away.
As for him,
He tipped his daily ash into
the dustbin every evening,
so began each morning with
his shirt and memory both freshly laundered
and never knew the clutter that she lived in.

To Mrs Ellis,
with sympathy . . .

Coral and Lester

Talk about grandeur,
and permanence too.
You felt there was no end to it
ever, in time or space,
looking up from below
at the sheer rock face.
Someone had carved three words at the base:
Coral loves Lester.
Perhaps she panicked there
in that ageless place.

Still life with people

They stood within the hard walls of my dream.
Not even a hair moved
from under the sleek hats. They'd all
slept well, been to the toilet and were
neither hungry nor thirsty nor dying.
In fact, they were all smiling complacently
so that I quickly framed the entire composition,
hung it in front of the window
and stood at a distance to admire the effect.

I remember my small grunt of
satisfaction that everyone was so
trim and organised without any kind of needs,
and I no longer had to keep open house for
crying people, straggling around
starving and dying untidily
in the soft parts of my brain.

Homo gestalt

Somewhere down the assembly line
somebody howled.
Nobody ran to help.
It wasn't the involuntary,
slightly incredulous cry
of a man who sees a finger
revolving independently in the machine
and dare not look at his hand.
They would have run then.
This was a different howl,
like a half-directed shudder,
a sigh-turned-howl, but
controlled by the mouth.
It would have been a roar but
the mouth, made smaller, round,
sifted and thinned it, maimed it,
until it howled in timid imitation
of a wolf, instead of bawling
like a man protesting.
Those who stood near him had heard
a yawn first,
a few bars of a popular song,
nothing, and then, as usual,
the howl, announcing a man
behind a machine
a man all day
five days a week
behind a machine.
Somewhere down the assembly line
a twin howl answered,
and suddenly the line was
a modulated chorus of howls
that stopped as suddenly,
and for half an hour there was glazed quiet.
Somewhere down the assembly line
somebody howled.
Nobody . . .

Semi-detached

She found a sprig of heather in the flower bed today.
The arms of the moor are reaching round the house
in which she waits
behind geraniums.
Her garden grows neatly still, organised on the surface
to keep the heath out and other ardours and arms
that might embrace the tamed plants,
uproot them,
restore them to the dark
possession of the moor. And yet
concealed by proper petals in the lawful flower bed
there is this sprig of the wild heath
that she alone saw
and left to grow there.

Evangelical Crusade

When the paradise of flesh has finally
withered behind locked bones,
behold! a Master comes
and stands before the disinherited,
arms outstretched, lips heavy, all
seduction in his stance, inviting
a permissible surrender of bodies
that have dutifully renounced the
real fruit.
In exchange this redeemer, this man
conjures up a divine imaginary apple
made of wax, complete with halo
and guaranteed for eternity.
So much for the future. For present
recompense a little ecstasy, a little
Christian orgy on the side, echoes of
old passions, of the genuine thing.
"I'm coming!" they shout,
and thrust their bodies forward to the hilt
in one long shuddering orgasm of guilt
and come, in their own hands.

Praying mantis

They don't fool me with talk of prayers.
It's obvious to anyone with half an eye
that its position is one of
love in action,
complete absence of prayer,
love that devours the lover in the act,
consumes him.
It's too close to home this,
disturbing—comforting to be able to
paralyse ourselves and it with prayers
and forget it.

Rep. for God & Co. Inc.

Levering slickly through kitchen doors
with slyly muttered lies about concerns
of health, or children, or saucepans,
depending on the case in hand,
the God rep. hawks his lurid policies
from house to house, his pale lips
sagging under heavy tales of
Last Judgements and
Hell beneath the garden plot.
Impassive walls of women don't deter him.
He extracts his sample God
from under layers of greasy patter
and, yelling "Behold Him!"
waves aloft a shop-soiled oddment of
a discontinued line, specially reduced
to suit all pockets,
three for the price of one.

Poet at a literary function

Hand in hand, they ran
away from the clutch of literary people,
the large teeth clattering and spattering
gems and dry biscuits in their wake.
Oh, they had to move fast to escape
the jaws of the righteous in cocktail dress.
But they had monstrous tubular blooms in mind
and bulbous dark plants with moist interiors,
cushioned warmly against the beaks
and considerable stones.
(These latter sought to pin them down to
polite peckings for literal corn.)
Once inside, safe in there where the sky is,
he stood up tall on a haystack with her beside him
and crowed a double triumph lustily
in superbly elegant bad taste.
Pure poetry.

The Interval

They were slow days. I drifted
with a slow complacency through
slow dreams. Two in my skin,
myself and a new generation,
out of the dated days
for the duration,
simply a few months' grace,
non-participation. I lived
as care-taker,
intent on my charge, coiled around it.
All my thoughts spiralled to the
thought within me,
cocooned it, layer upon layer,
glazing my eyes to watchers,
muffling my ears.
This gathering commotion claimed my living,
absorbed identity within my dream.

Genesis

I'm sorry, I said,
I don't usually behave like this,
and it seemed the thing to say.
But that was before,
that was when there was only
pain and fear and
May I scream? I asked
but they said no,
so I held it behind my teeth
where it slowly spread.
It spread all through me,
hard and swelling,
till the membrane night closed round me,
taut. I had to suffocate or
burst, and
there was light, and
May I sleep? I asked
and they said yes.

Child with fairy floss

He turned to me, accusing me,
the giver of giftless gifts, and
thrust the other half into my hand,
deceived,
his first taste of the refined pleasure
of having and yet not having
leaving him rather grumpy.
No doubt he will cultivate a taste for it
with practice.

Child with flowers

There you go,
netting flowers with your glance,
holding their gold lightly
in filaments of sunlight reflected from
your eyes. They are all
yours, little breeze,
tiny plant-charmer, yours to
touch, caress. You conjure
blossoms out of hiding and
laugh at them,
squander them richly
like sunshine. For you they are
no more precious than diamonds
or water. They are,
simply,
as you are.
How you accept their sudden presence.
How you accept yourself,
small butterfly decked in
such flimsy muslin.

Child in moonlight

Such miracles are yours still,
performed in your bright eyes,
but how shall I protect you from
the neat word, the whittler
that slinks its way even into
the vast deep at the word's end
to pare your broken moon
to requisite dimensions of
crescent dreariness
until its light goes out?
How shall I protect your kindled eyes
from the voluble dark?
Who will stay silent enough,
wordless enough
at the word's end?

Suffer little children

The adult congregation
professed they had caught god
in their own image,
in the self-respecting varnish,
in the ten-commandment faces
stranded high on Sunday collars
propped on pin-stripes, righteously
suffering little children.

They believed they had condensed him
in the Word, oozing
unctuously round plastic flowers,
dipping in the water-jug
and reappearing, heavily
sodden, depressing.

They hoped the walls contained him,
chapel-pallid surfaces entombing
the damp thud of dead prayer.
And the children were bursting to plunge
in the roar of the wind outside,
and the children suffered.

Suicide

He would have preferred to live
but there are some for whom
living is not easy.
It has to be learned—
the sliding smile,
the whipping speech,
the careless hearing.
Some children never learn
and he was one
who shot himself,
the balance of his mind
still undisturbed.

Butterflies

All that long, dark hatching for
an odd flutter or two, just to be able to
make an entrance and an exit,
almost on the same breath.
As if they weren't there for their own purposes
at all, but as decoration,
to be seen from the outside,
in multitudes.
As if alone they had no meaning
except the one we like to give them,
from the outside.
I've seen men crush butterflies,
and others, more desperate still, preserve them,
pinned down dead in long rows in cemeteries.

Elderly citizens' mystery tour

Caught in the engine's torrent,
their bodies sweep past, neck deep,
and only their struggling eyes
grasp at trailing creepers as they pass.
All the quick-flash flickering reels
of slippery, gum-glossy trees
project no shape to cling to.
and yet they knew the earth once
stock still beneath their feet
and they took for granted the fact of a rock,
ignored its crumbly texture,
never doubted their hold on ropy trees
that drowning arms remember.

Age of Reason

These pine trees once hid reasonable fears,
familiar giants of my childhood years.
Since then the world has grown, I've stood
in cavernous, black, threatening aisles
of Queensland's sodden forests, seen
mad gum trees slithering up to high
pot-holes of light, wreathed silently
with damply waiting leaves, and heard
the whip-birds' startled, catapulting cry
drop yelping down from far grey disks of sky
to smother ages deep in writhing, thin
tendrils of vine, where echoing screams begin.
Dark theories worm into my giant mind,
cadaverous exile lurking in the pines.

Integrated

Immigrant indeed.
She brought her country with her
in packing-cases.
Rocking to the sound of a sousta
from the gram. as she shouts advice
to her daughter in the tongue
of her youth, she affirms that
she has not migrated.
All around she hears and sees
the trappings of her Cretan home—
the shopkeeper, her nephew; the priest
who comes for coffee,
the children, casks of oil, the cups and cupboards,
even vines, all
except the donkeys and the white taverna,
and these her vivid memory supplies.
Her grandchild, playing near her, sees
wattle, leafy mango trees,
poinsettia in bloom, hears
kookaburras,
pop-songs from the radio,
has eaten corned-beef, cornflakes,
reads the comics,
knows the beach and coca-cola rounds,
another tongue, her future.
The grandmother believes in integration.
After the fierce initial confrontation,
the land gave way, she arranged it to her liking.
Australia is more malleable than she.

Immigrant

He played ping-pong, abashed,
though he didn't show it,
at sniggers from his future countrymen,
immaculate in careful shipboard shorts.
Back home in Thessaly he always wore
pyjamas in the house,
work-clothes at work,
his Sunday suit on Sundays
and other holidays.
On board the ship, being neither at his work
nor home, he wore his Sunday suit
to undertake ping-pong between two worlds.

To a poet's anxious girl-friend

No wonder you're concerned.
Who wouldn't be?
Now it's in its early stages but,
like drink,
drugs
and other furtive vices,
it's liable to get a hold on him
and end up colouring his life.

It starts like this—merely
belated adolescent bravado or
compensation for a nervous twitch or stammer.
At first it's only once a week, but soon it's
every day and finally
nights too.
He'll burn holes in the plastic walls of your tidy dreams
and let the wind in
if you don't watch him.

Besides which he's liable to
give up mothballs,
eat the telly,
grow his hair and fingers and
install kaleidoscopes on hire purchase.
What begins as a spare-time hobby
will eventually affect his senses,
and yours (it's contagious).

So all in all I'd advise you to
stay clear of the man
unless you can
get him to have treatment before it goes any further.
In its later stages it's terrible and
quite incurable.

Roots

They suffocate your poems, bury your bones
and stick a cross on you to cross you out,
dead dissident in whose wide-open eyes
they saw themselves
 ugly.
 But the roots.
They forget the roots
that delve down deep into their native earth
at night
and spread there, tunnelling secretly
underground,
waiting
to push up new shoots quietly to the light
in some forgotten wood.
And in the warm spring days,
unheeded,
the shoots will flower into blood-red poems,
releasing all their arsenal of seeds
in new minds,
waiting.
Then will the living offspring of your death
grow tall and watchful, guardians of light,
throwing down roots again
ready for next time
and the next time . . .

In the beginning

Hot in the throat of man stung, eventually,
A Word,
and he spat it out, proudly watched it
hissing away from him in flames;
then, cooling, it grew
round and bloated, circling
self-importantly, inevitably
begetting generations of words, clinging
greyly in cold galaxies of clichés,
ash of the primary fire,
representing a drab order,
imposing it,
censoring visions and dreams,
prepared to inherit the earth.

Leap-froggers' waltz

When words come leaping and hiccupping
from cavernous places
and others crowd behind, echoing already,
announcing their arrival from
deep dark in the well of me,
when they come with open arms in their voices,
shouting or laughing, spitting
or copulating incestuously,
some ugly and poxed, others fat and blooming,
but all strange, a motley grouping
frogging
from the well of me,
I let them be;
they choke if they're laced in the genteel stays
of prosody. But sometimes,
trying to please, they mince out
dancing grotesquely in waltz-time,
which is very polite and nice of them
and, fortunately, rare.

By their poems ye shall know them: Poem

All I know about poetry is that it has
something to do with sex,
something very close to sex,
polarised sex—
all the words erect and pointing
in one direction—urgent—
or not urgent in the least but
ponderous and heavy with
slow rhythms and long, deep sighs.
Others prefer craft,
making an art of it, delicately and with
fine workmanship interweaving
bodies in words
lovingly.
Some poems fall anyhow,
all of a heap anywhere, dishevelled,
legs apart in loneliness and
desperation,
and there's talk about standards.

Bananas and Elders

I remember one banana
above all others.
Peeled, it looked pale
and every-day as margarine
before they coloured it buttercup,
yet what the teeth met of succulence
in the first, soft bite
was rare enough to build a childhood dream on.
And all that melting in a golden sheath
of most unfruit-like shape—
to one accustomed to crab-apples
in rationed England.

I made it last all day.

For years afterwards it fed visions
of a banana-tree glade, all shade,
a little, secret hollow scooped in
stooped banana trees
where I could eat bananas all day long
only for lifting an arm and picking them.
A dream amongst the homely elder trees
that twisted gnarled, dry branches
round my wishing.

I've seen them now—
banana trees—
too late to bend and curl
around me, caressing.
They're plain and stiff as feather mops,
unmysterious: their once forbidden fruit
has lost its savour with the eating.
Somehow those little, wizened elders
contained the mystery.
Theirs was the mellow, secret sap
that nourished the ripening dream.

Renewed acquaintance

Accidentally, I dropped my grey tome
squarely onto a toe.
It yelled, I watched it wriggling,
and as one thing leads to another, next
I saw a foot, it
kicked the book and
I kissed my arms and bit them,
peeled myself to the skin all over,
stood in front of a mirror and laughed,
recognising my body at last
elbowing out of my mind
and laughing welcome back,
welcome.

Consider the lily-bombs

Moving so fast now, only my eyes
stare through smoke as I pass by, wildly
dropping live poems along my route,
expecting them to explode into
considerable paper lilies and hook someone
behind me with their tongues
so that if I pass this way again
we might meet, spinning,
on a lily stalk,
anchored on great petals with paper tooth-spikes
till the colour changes and it's time for
another round on a new record.
I'll never meet these poems again.
I throw them out of the window,
go deaf and
get out regularly at the next revolution.

Creation

Today is virgin still, unmoulded,
not yet remembered,
and my last image shattered at your door.
Here I wait,
smooth and innocent as potter's clay,
an embryonic swan or hunchbacked lizard.
This is the white suspense before creation
when all we know is now.
I can become, this moment,
shaped by your quick hands.
Tomorrow my collecting past
will range the new creation
amongst the figurines that qualify me.
Tomorrow will interpret this blind hour.
Today I have no memory to brand me.

Night journey

I felt my way towards you in the dark through
alien lands wasted and worn after long drought.
Years away. The futile moon waxed and waned dementedly
behind thick clouds as I stumbled on, avoiding pits,
hands groping for my feet to trip me, hold me
out of your sight for ever. I could not see you,
could not come to where you were easily.
What snares I skirted that night you will never know,
searching for you, faltering along crumbling ledges
towards your waiting presence suddenly,
stone giant shape against the sky,
stars behind you, granite looming strange and huge
in such din of silence. Fearless at last I ran,
regardless of all danger, and stood before you offering
my scarred throat, my sightless eyes fixed
on where your face should be, my torn and jagged mind
clawing at the night that yielded only
your outline. Frenzied, I tore up roots, willing
chasms into existence, prepared
for all things, one word,
the full flood of light
or the abyss.

Dream's end

Long hours poised
on the edge of your second coming. No
return to the dark lands. Even now
I see the sun's arms reaching through old clouds
towards this hill where I stand naked
in buttercups to receive you, real, striding
through the tall grass of my perfected dream.
Here shall I worship you, your hair,
your face devoid of shadow, transfiguration
on the mount of buttercups, holy
revelation of sunlight flooding into
the stone circle of our pagan love.

* * *

I welcome you as the parched earth welcomes
rain after a long drought,
as sunflowers open to the sun
and follow its course with their long gaze.
I welcome you as woman welcomes man,
secretly, into the valley of her deep need,
hushed under banked clouds. Here I
cast a spell between your breath and mine
invoking the unfathomable storm to break and
drown me irretrievably in your love.

Foxglove

This shall be remembered—
a rock-lined hollow where the earth lies
damp and secret under deep green, all green
except for you and me and one extraordinary foxglove,
one extraordinary foxglove.
This shall be remembered and the wind,
too high to touch us, moving on without us,
hidden deep dark on the damp earth
with ferns and nettles, your liquid face,
your heart on mine, mysteriously
sealed in a green underworld with
one outrageous foxglove.
This shall be remembered in pale
seasons though we should die even
to each other—
this deep place, this touch, this long
silence of ferns,
this naked flower growing from the earth,
this foxglove,
this vulnerable foxglove.

Seaside Idyll

Lying on the beach envying paired gulls—
"Crows fly too," you said—and I, who had passed
the afternoon millenium dissolving quietly into sand
at your side, met your suggestion head-on, staggered
my eyes around to see your gaze cowled,
turned inward on a starker consummation.
The convoluted sea lay dark and restless,
preparing to uncoil, take, enfold, disturbing
only the sand.
Singular crows advanced across the sky,
lacerating light.

* * *

I await the new dimensions of our existence
like bird in rosy temple. I wait
looking out through ribs of shadow
into the orange east which probed its pale fingers
deep into my opening shell. I wait,
prepared for all things, all kingdoms come
on earth, all heaven in your eyes' hearth.
I wait. I await you, fire of my soul,
blood's force, river of liquid sunrise
called to my distant shore. I await you
poised in chaos of shifting winds and seas,
all anchorage dissolved. I await
your touch,
your breath,
your universe
gold as corn and glowing in the embers of a dream.

Love, first

Aimer d'abord. Il sera toujours temps ensuite de s'interroger sur ce qu'on aime jusqu'à n'en vouloir plus rien ignorer.

André Breton

I dare not look at you
for fear my eyes should burn
from too much light, too close,
too soon.
If I could touch your hand, our eyes
averted, and feel your blood swell
crimson in the dark towards
my shore . . . If I could feel
your breath's lick, your tongue
on mine, your heart on
my heart, hair in my hair . . .
If I could feel you flooding through
the long, primeval night of
my veins, shaping hills and valleys
with your waves, could hear
the earth's pulse thudding
in the caves of our embrace,
oh then, my love, would be the time
to call for light,
and more light,
to look upon the world that we had made.

Intimacy

Fear
of the closeness that blinds.
If you could stand away a little
perhaps I could distinguish who you are,
and others too would be discernible,
not over your shoulder-
a mirage of cavorting specks
beyond your blinding shadow-
but full-length people, arms bare,
made of flesh and love, afraid.
Sadness
that there's no time to clasp
the world beyond us.
The scattering of emotion we could spare
is far too sparse to yield.
It's two or loneliness.
We are condemned
to love up close, obscuring,
hoping
that through the dark penumbra
of each other lies salvation.
No time to move away a little,
and your eyes so close to mine
I cannot even see you.

Independent

We slept on mother earth that night,
body to sod,
and I, for one, felt it, firmer than flesh
and safer,
a less precarious balance.
For that night I no longer needed you.
I neither gave nor asked for a response.
The earth was enough—
hard, unfeeling, barren—
but it lay still all night,
never turned nor complained
nor felt the weight of me
unbearable.
I was a layer between the earth and stars,
could lift a finger, touch,
or blot them out.

Love

Writhing with soft emblems of hopeful eglantine
my mind breaks out of the flowery hollow of your dreams
and sucks your heart out.
You are there but there is no covering the
long distance of proximity that would bring me
under your breath,
under your tongue,
inside the tent of you where
warts are and bubbles.
Under the steaming canopy of your
turkish-bath chest, closed in with
fur and mosquitoes and all the laughing hyenas
of hysterical waiting at last,
rice will grow under our very noses while we
perform our fierce ritual,
killing each other with hate,
over and over.

Boots

Here you come with your big boots on
and my invisible heart lurches out of the window
to greet you. My unreal hands tug, hopelessly,
at nothing, your big boots,
stuck in a sink of dishes,
tenderly, oh so tenderly stroking
your thighs, your calves, offering
my overcrowded life to your homing legs,
kneeling before you, altars
in my imaginary, impotent head.

Round

Here the daily dream repeats itself daily
with the milkman.
There's something desolate about
an empty bottle.
Rice Bubbles trickle down the window-pane
recalling nights spent
trapped in the same dream,
floating through the garden with a
fire-extinguisher,
putting the flowers out.
(Their colours created a bright fury in her head,
leaving too much to chance as butterflies do.)
Did you remember to switch the birds off darling?
Yes. Goodnight.
(Repeat)

A Warning

If I were real I would come to you now, naked
in the half-light of your love.
I would simply smile and ask this or that of you,
would hold you, gently,
not wildly, crazed, wanting to
crush you into my bones,
dry, dry dust on the dead earth.
Perhaps I shall take you with me
into my tomb. Perhaps I shall
strangle you with my cold need. The green
has left the trees, the earth
dried, barren. The wind
takes all that is given, all. You,
I shall fade your colours. I shall
suck you dry, dry dust in my grave.
I shall lock you in bone unless
you are very strong, unless
you are so strong and green, flooding
river of life, and I can drink,
drink endlessly and grow new and real
on your earth.

Survival

Mummies, skins of dried passions preserved in darkness,
await daylight only to disintegrate completely.
Instant decay: a small explosion gives the wind its own.
Your words embalm breath, seal me in cryptic confinement.
I beat the walls, the ceiling. Your tears, collapsing,
fill my mouth with ashes. Nails
claw for air, tearing
your flesh. My desiccated skull
butts, thrusts
and bursts newborn into dissolvent light.

Out of step

Today your eyes discovered mine, too late.
I have abducted you into my brain.
Your image in the hot-house of my head
is far more real than real,
more fleshed with the material stuff
of dreams and poems and love
than is your presence.
Within the fertile hollows of my lust
I graft you secretly to my desire,
conceiving demons, legacies of fear
once visited on Lilith by patriarchal man
to hide his shame.
And now your eyes court mine too late,
so how shall I explain
that I have learnt to murder real men
to feed the changeling growing in my brain.

Solar system

I cannot reach you now, Love.
You have become, for me,
a distant point of sunlight
cocooned in night.
Slowly my dreaming poems revolve around you,
pale progeny of fire
unable to approach, nor yet escape
this orbit of desire.
My cooling poems weave circles round the sun,
their source, their point of focus,
their kingdom come,
and gone.

Awakening to snow

Blades of light slide under my eyelids
and prise them open to discover
softness.
This is whisper day, muffled in deep down
of eiderdown snow, day of
those other echoes and shadows on frosted window-panes
that pass by furtively, wondering.
Today is hushed blue day of nothing, of
empty footprints where feet were,
of absence.
Today adrift from all the gongs of time,
suspended on the feather of your
silent white breath.

Stripped

Fancy-dress won't do.
In the end things work through
the paper covering to the bone.
Wrap your garland words around you,
decorate your eyes and ears—the sun
glares, curls the edges,
wilts the cosy wreaths;
shrivelled words fall off
and leave you naked in your bones,
your lovely golden bones,
your airy lookout.

The truth of the matter

Having only lately become accustomed
to seeing them, I still find them strange
and very wonderful, these
rocks that dissolve into arms,
eyes in wood,
thundering torrents of life
composed of the soluble dead—
these ears a scattered bird-call
in the tangled hair of the wind,
while from this unreal hand
real sunflowers thrust—
ashes to fountains
and dust to improbable seeds
from which improbable worlds
continue to burst.

Not with a bang

A big bang was needed, an explosion.
We knew it and we used to think ourselves
capable of it, finally, when we'd gathered the energy.
But we know now that all the little fizzles
we nurtured once as harbingers
are really what's to be expected of us,
the entire thing.
Like jumping-jacks around the bonfire,
crack and fizzle, aping
miniature bombs, in little spurts,
insignificantly spluttering
in order to jump back in our own ash
and fizzle out.

Correspondent

You I meet only on paper—
long, sinuous coils of paper that
wind towards each other in
blue distances and embrace like lilies
of remembrance.
I think our letters hold hands piously
out there where the wind breaks,
where neither you nor I will ever venture
because the atmosphere is too rarefied
for people. Only letters meet there,
smoke-signals of our lives, that disperse
carelessly in any old passing breeze.
But your spit on the envelope stands out solid
and opaque in all this transparency of incense,
comfortable, a reminder of
stained hands and clumsy hearts that
pump real blood.

Head-on

Bumping into
a moment of confusion today
I had to dig you out of a chaos of
falling plaster and all-coloured hair.
I finally recognised you,
man in a face in a name emerging
from the ashes of my head after
one of those sudden collisions,
making us lose our footing like that and
tumble off the tight-rope of immediate intentions
into each other's world.
It took all morning to
climb back up here again.

"yes and shadows"
(for Tom Shapcott)

And afterwards seasons become
horizontal containers marked fragile
for carrying fragile people
in the fourth season.

Now the rain spears
and shoots up shattering
into light

yes and shadows.
You are light
diviner

under the humpbacked shadows
astride your four shoulders,
squeezing it into strange shapes
that ooze like plasticine between
your rain fingers.

I hear the light thudding
like mud on glass
blocking out shadows
like silence.

It's hard to hold on to that
with this astride my back, this frog,
thumping my shoulder-blades
with every breath
in grass outside that light,
outside that rain.
I'm the frog now, I fuse like
shadows in grass with other shadows.
Cold. The sky is ebbing away
in there where the people were
singing.
The fourth season is about to congeal
in my blood alone, my throat,
scored with grappling hooks that
missed the wall and suspended me to myself.

Recoil

I've withdrawn my wounded feelers,
pulled them in,
I've drawn up my knees to my chin,
wrapped myself in my own tentacular arms
and buried my fingers deep in my own skin.
A mad position they say,
a singular form of madness.

Empty house

Here the house waits formlessly for
neighbours and other fillers of doorways
who will contend that all is well
and keep the wind out.
Against them I can bounce confidently
back into shape again
from the far corners of the house,
but in the meantime there is this
grey shifting of shadows,
there is unrelatedness, slow
dissolution of memory, clothes, bed,
these things that define me.
In the long spaces between neighbours
there is a shapeless lurking in corners,
there is nothing
except the danger of draughts.

A dustbin is an ashcan

Death to the funeral parlours and their stench of
decomposing curtains and flowers.
What we need are
candy-striped removal vans and
re-usable family coffins of hard-wearing polythene,
with pedal-lid,
good for an infinite number of dumpings
and flittings.

It's time to deflower death,
rape it, stick a stupid coffin in the hall
and use it to
stuff our souls and rubbish in,
pillage it, rip off its fancy ornaments
to decorate our beds.
Children could play games of
grandmothers and grandfathers on its
pink satin lining
and cats could litter there.
As for men and women, how splendid,
how violently real and alive their bodies would be
within laughing range of a
comical, naked coffin.

The lady burns books

They burn, they burn, books,
paper forests of a mind grown dark
and complex, huge with coiled thoughts
waiting to spring at her.
Poor eyes. Poor wanderers searching
other people's worlds for paths they recognise,
for pits with snakes (and worms)
to burn them out.
For these she knows. They loiter
on the dark side of her eyes at night,
waiting
to penetrate her Dresden china dreams
and writhe with her, consenting, in the mud
of some black pit deeper than desire,
primeval, slimy Eden impervious to fire.

Sunday in the Midlands

Long Sunday intervenes, creeps in
null and void while we're not looking
and haunts us. The mind
slips to low voltage and we begin the
slow motion of unrelated acts we shan't remember
on Monday. The day passes somewhere
else, begins
somehow and ends
at some time in the future conditional, but when
it starts and ends exactly we can't
say, we can't
catch it in the act. Uncertainty
reflected from some forgotten dream,
Sunday lingers, formless, in the brain,
neither coming nor going,
clouding earth and sky
without shadow. On this
pale screen there is no yesterday. Tomorrow
is nowhere. We wait
for images, touchstones of our presence here, some
evidence. Anything
is possible, but
nothing ever happens on Sunday.

The Passion

Once there were other gods. Now
she has dreamed a Christ of her desire,
clothing him in flesh for long hot nights of
ecstasy, of Word incarnate. Her body
opens to her phantom lover, risen up erect
from sleeping death to enter her.
Holy ghost.
She is not so simple. She knows
what eating bread and drinking wine can lead to,
later, hammered to the cross of her own need
with the terrible deep nails of supreme agony.
The husband lies beside his whimpering wife
and swears he'll crucify this incubus, this
mutant Jupiter, this wayward bull conceived
for other purposes than this (he thought)
and bury him deep next time, too deep
for resurrection,
with all his clothes on.

Libraries

No wonder we whisper here.
Seekers after specialised delights to be performed
deep in the secret sanctum of the brain
we edge along walls, furtively sniffing
musky rows of books, fingering
other people's dreams, hoping for
rare contact beyond flesh,
more cultured,
more cultivated.
Our searching hands meet membranes,
feelers, umbilical cords,
dabble in pale secretions, damp,
voluptuous linings of minds exposed
for disembodied intercourse. In these temples
of refined lust our haunted ghosts mate
with other ghosts,
spiralling desperately on smoke-signals of
incense and absence.

Nymphomania

If I were a man I would be
tenderness, I would lick
your body, but woman I am wild
and my pointed teeth always seek out flesh
to spite myself and your ears.
What will you do without ears?
How shall we make love
without ears?

My hand grovels and claws in your mouth
to tear out words of love with your dead tongue and
I search for you there in the empty tomb of your eyes.
Monster, Monstress I am pregnant with a fearful need
that will never be born
but holds me still nailed in anguish
to the bed of your belly cross
And I wait
And I wait
And I wait.

Mirage

You dropped into the centre of my sleep
and all night long the circles of your presence grew
until my dream was all of you, my blood
invaded so that I could bring you with me
into morning.
And all day long I've functioned
on the outskirts of my mind
while, folded in, I held your features safe, waiting
to write them into substance, into light.
But all these other voices, small concerns,
these bird-songs, these leaves and suppositions
have gradually encroached upon the dream,
diminishing its power to occupy
all but the central kernel of my mind,
too dark to see, your features
all forgotten, your tenderness a memory of sun.
Oh my strange lover will I never give you form?
How many dreams of you have gone astray, dissolved
into vague longing, this
regret, these phantom poems reaching back through deserts
to a mirage.

The sublimation cycle

There was a time when your name hovered round
my lips all day and, during sleep,
found substance in my breath. But that was
long ago. Now you have joined the shadows
of my head, those nameless longings that
eclipse my mind and send me prowling, howling
silently through dead streets in search of something
lost, almost forgotten, probing strangers' eyes. And then
the poem comes, throbbing, from somewhere deep
inside, orgastic pain
seeking deliverance only to be absorbed again,
filtered back through my own veins
and left transmuted, shadow in my brain.

Fused

The city's dark skin, stretched out taut
under a tattoo of feet, offers precarious balance
to the shoppers, their robot eyes connected to lights,
geared to new barter of beads and trappings.
These silent hunters climb in elevators, single
minds retracted, impervious to presences, mechanically
pressing buttons, waiting. But when
the lift stops, nowhere, and a sudden night
reveals its cage of strangers in intimate embrace,
pressed thigh against thigh, breast against breast,
all steely certainty of self dissolves, flesh
seeks reassurance, calls
sister, calls brother, fuses
identity in one black, arbitrary second out of time,
suspended,
till someone screams.
Under our feet the jungle stirs a little.

Ice Age

Come, but here I offer no soft cushion
for you to lie hair on down, no jellied waves
to tremble and suck warmly at your shore,
moulding your flesh to mine.
If you will join me on my sheet of hard clarity
it is only for vistas of plate-glass and crystal,
arrested waterfalls slow as the steady stalactites
of my want.
For I am mad with a cold passion that holds me
prisoner in stainless glass, glazing my stiffened eyeballs
to your need. Here there are sheer cubes,
mirrors, splinters of ice, here
grasp the stamens of my brittle blood
precisely timed to swell and crack my veins
as soon as the thaw sets in.

Pagan

Here in England in summer a billow of soft trees
cushions the sharp edges of mind, imposing
surrender. I yield to comfort, the luxury of
deep green pile, sink thanklessly into grassy hollows of
thought with only a small memory of
something left behind in the cold,
the crystalline indicator of a stark concern,
splinter of dry ice trained on images of
crossed branches, dead in a dead sky.
A hopeless cycle of symbols claws relentlessly
at pale veins, promising now death,
now life, the fall from grace, the winter,
the Easter resurrection of the trees. Forced
gratitude to someone and always, in every
new season, a new retribution for artificial sins
erodes the harmonious dream.
The carefully preserved ice of my clarity
melts now, irresistibly, in the heat of this spontaneous
rebirth, and I am almost ready again to forget
some uncalled-for intervention in the proud flow
of my blood's seasons, some sacrificial insult to
my pagan understanding, somewhere along the way.

A fall of angels

Only a short time ago there was
an upward movement, a soaring of new wings
sunward. Summer billowed and lapped softly
at high noon, spiralling thistledown, aspirations,
eagles.
Two shadows passed before the sun, briefly,
a meaningless phenomenon, reflections in grass,
in water; birds shrieked regardless and wheeled
a high course, edging the safe contour of sky,
a form of challenge.
Everything is possible, love, eternity,
forget-me-nots, the sun, old hardy perennial.
Everything is possible for angels on heat. Amnesia.
Easy to forget that leaves have their seasons,
flowers start to peel, the mind to slough off
summer, admitting mist
at the back of the eyeballs. How they turn
downward, falling away now, all those spring words
disguised as evergreens, turning and fading
and falling. Clear the lawns, the pathways,
make bonfires, make way
for the cold season, dead sunflowers, damp
eagles' wings that nearly touched the sun
and yield now to the earth's dull pull,
this owlish consummation. Leaves and spent rockets
fizzle out ingloriously in somebody's back garden,
a seasonal happening, a clumsy fall of angels.

Last year's poem

Last year's poem,
cast off like a skin and therefore,
presumably, decaying
even then,
looks strange now with the return of
another spring,
hooked dry and lifeless on a
dead bush,
completely unconnected with
this year's slick new me.